GIVE THIS MAN

SOME COLOR

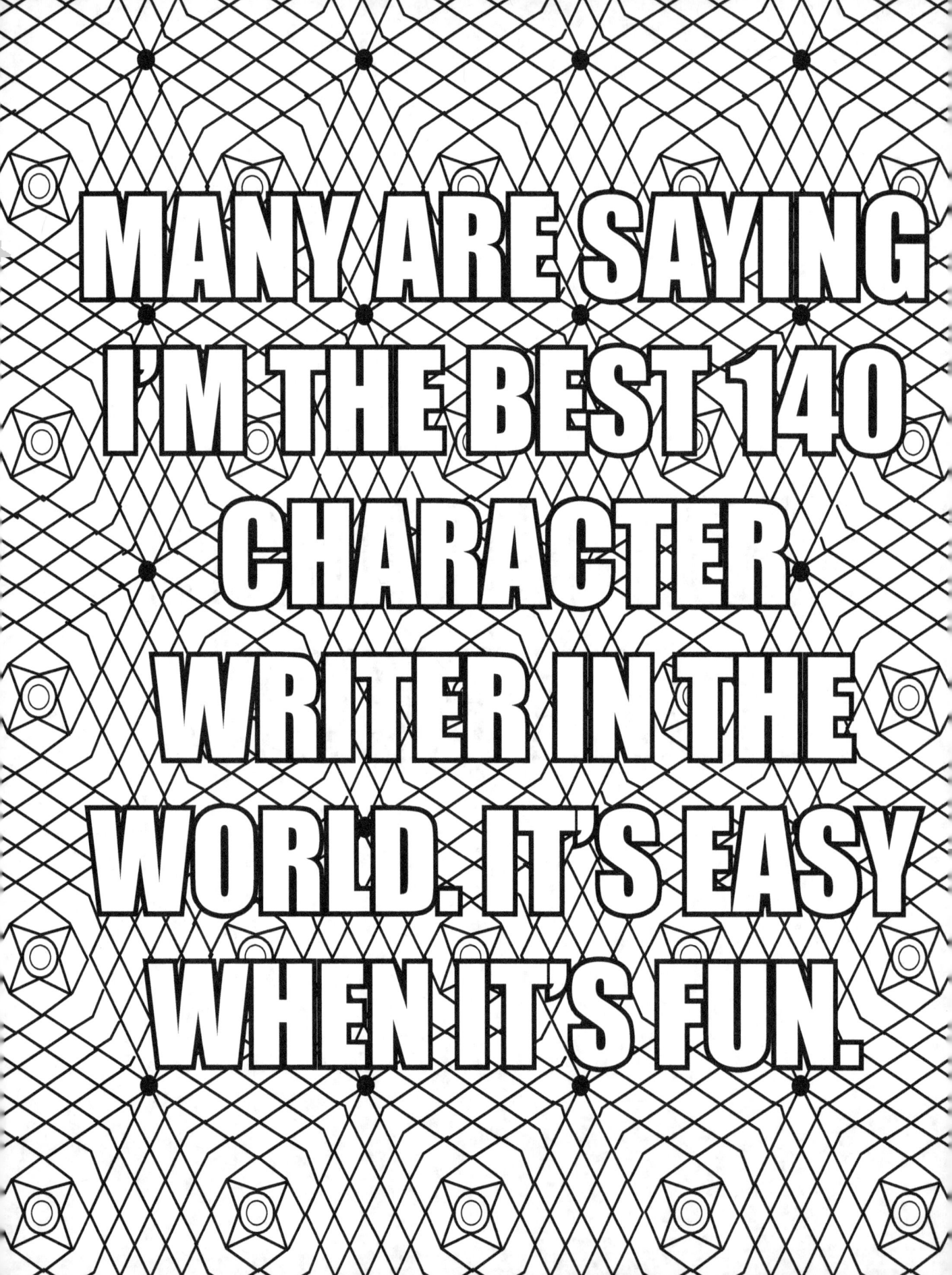

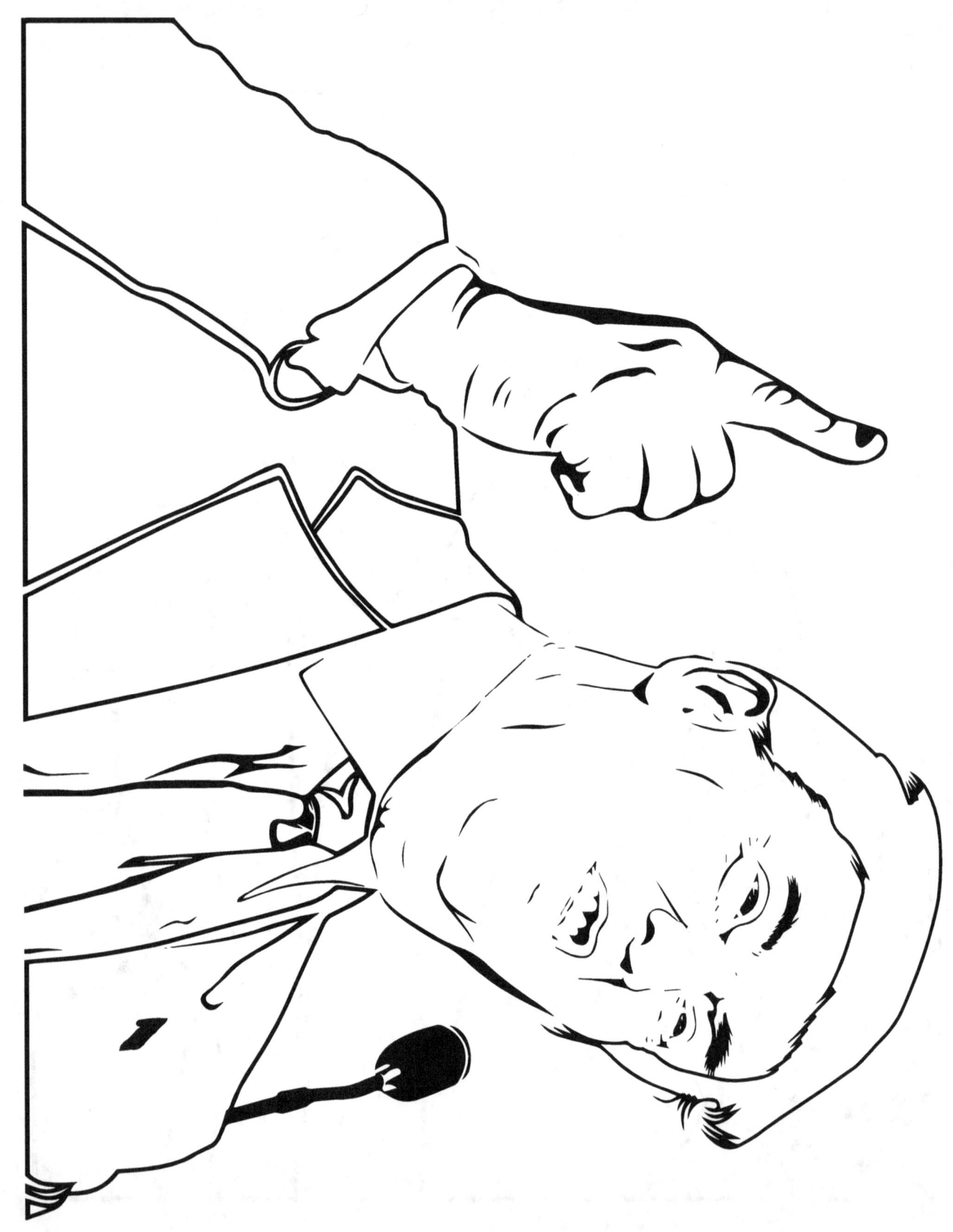

THE CONCEPT OF GLOBAL WARMING WAS CREATED BY AND FOR THE CHINESE IN ORDER TO MAKE U.S. MANUFACTURING NON-COMPETITIVE.

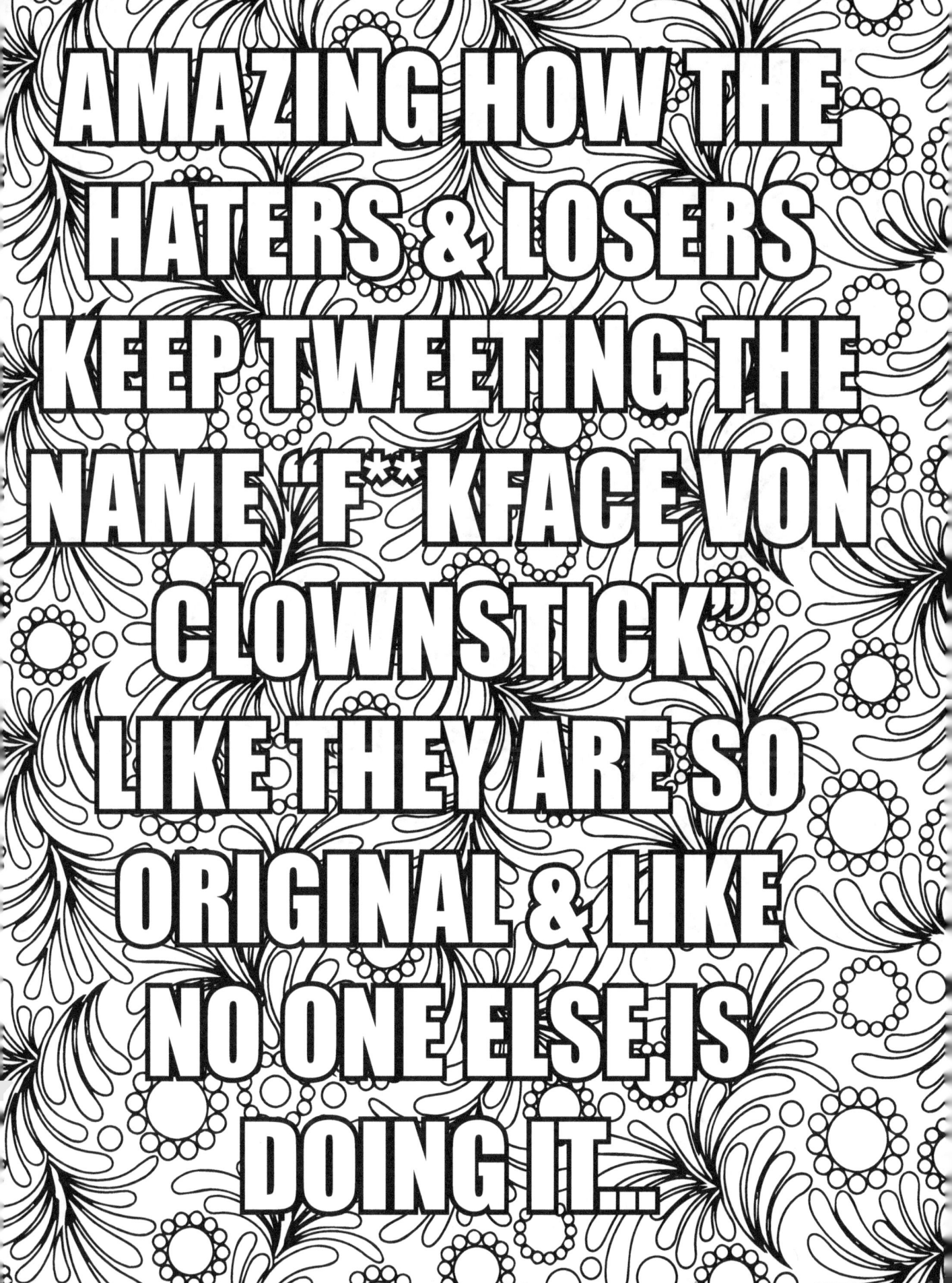

AMAZING HOW THE HATERS & LOSERS KEEP TWEETING THE NAME "F**KFACE VON CLOWNSTICK" LIKE THEY ARE SO ORIGINAL & LIKE NO ONE ELSE IS DOING IT....

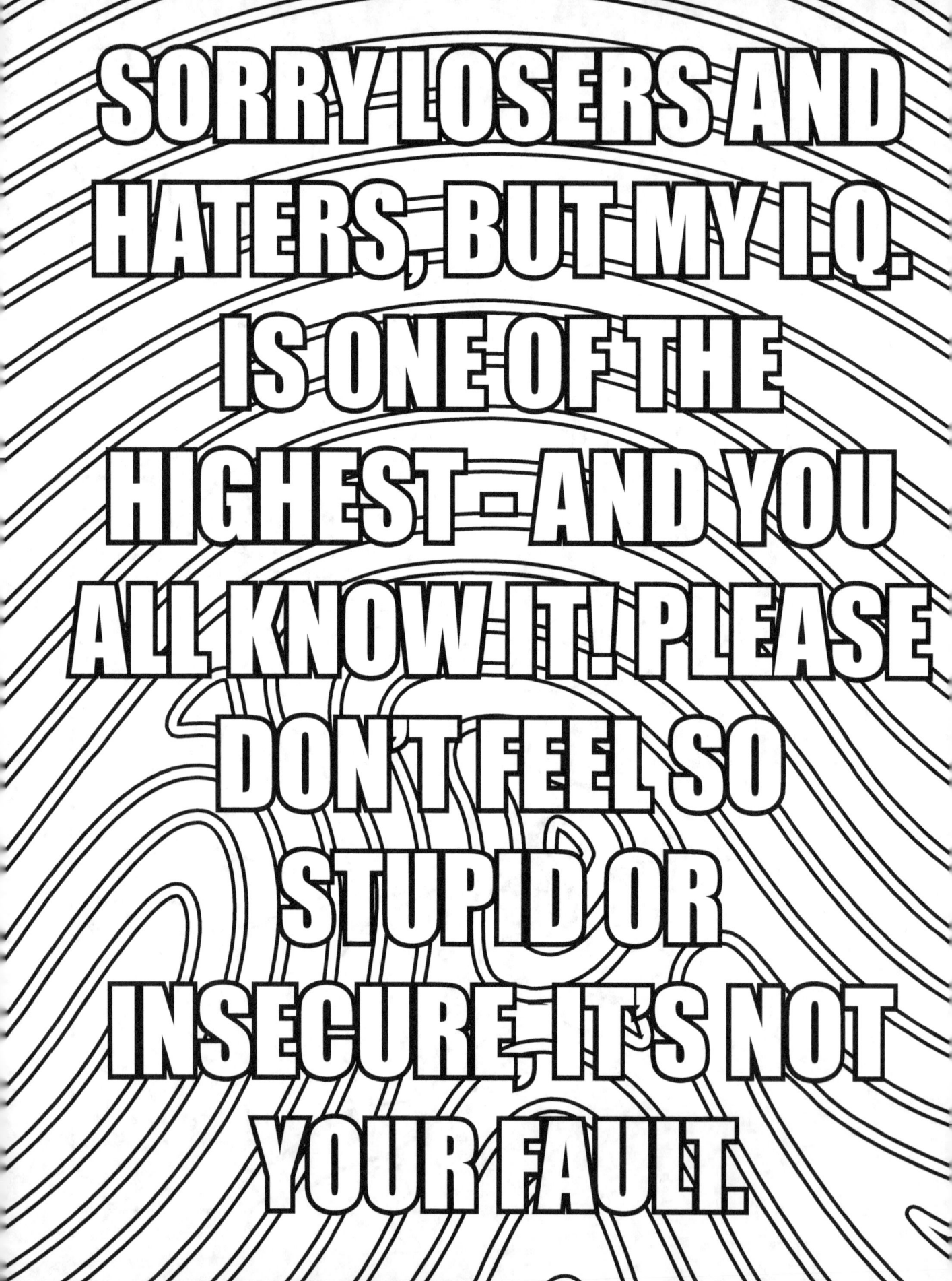

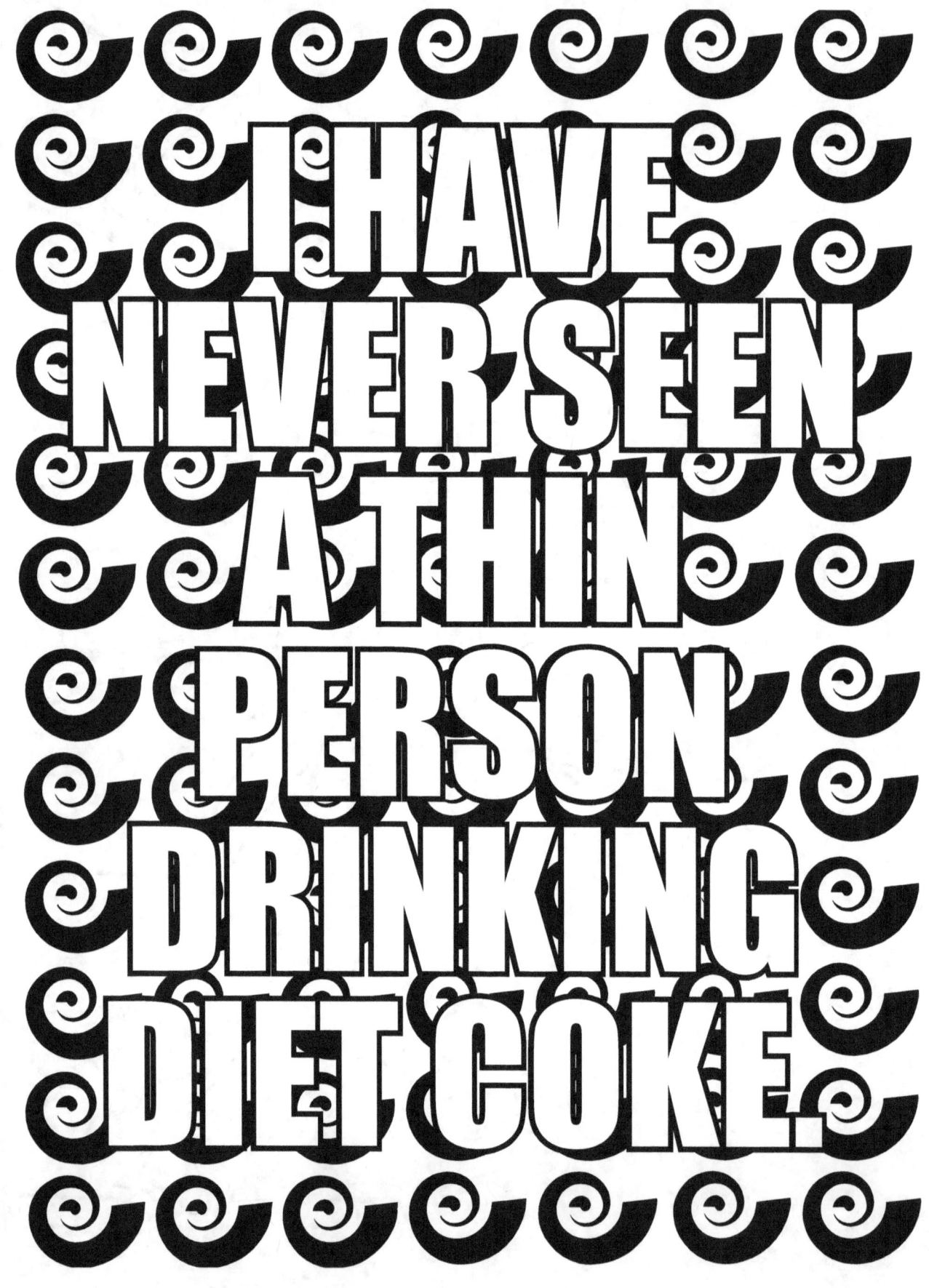

I WOULD LIKE TO EXTEND MY BEST WISHES TO ALL, EVEN THE HATERS AND LOSERS, ON THIS SPECIAL DATE, SEPTEMBER 11TH.

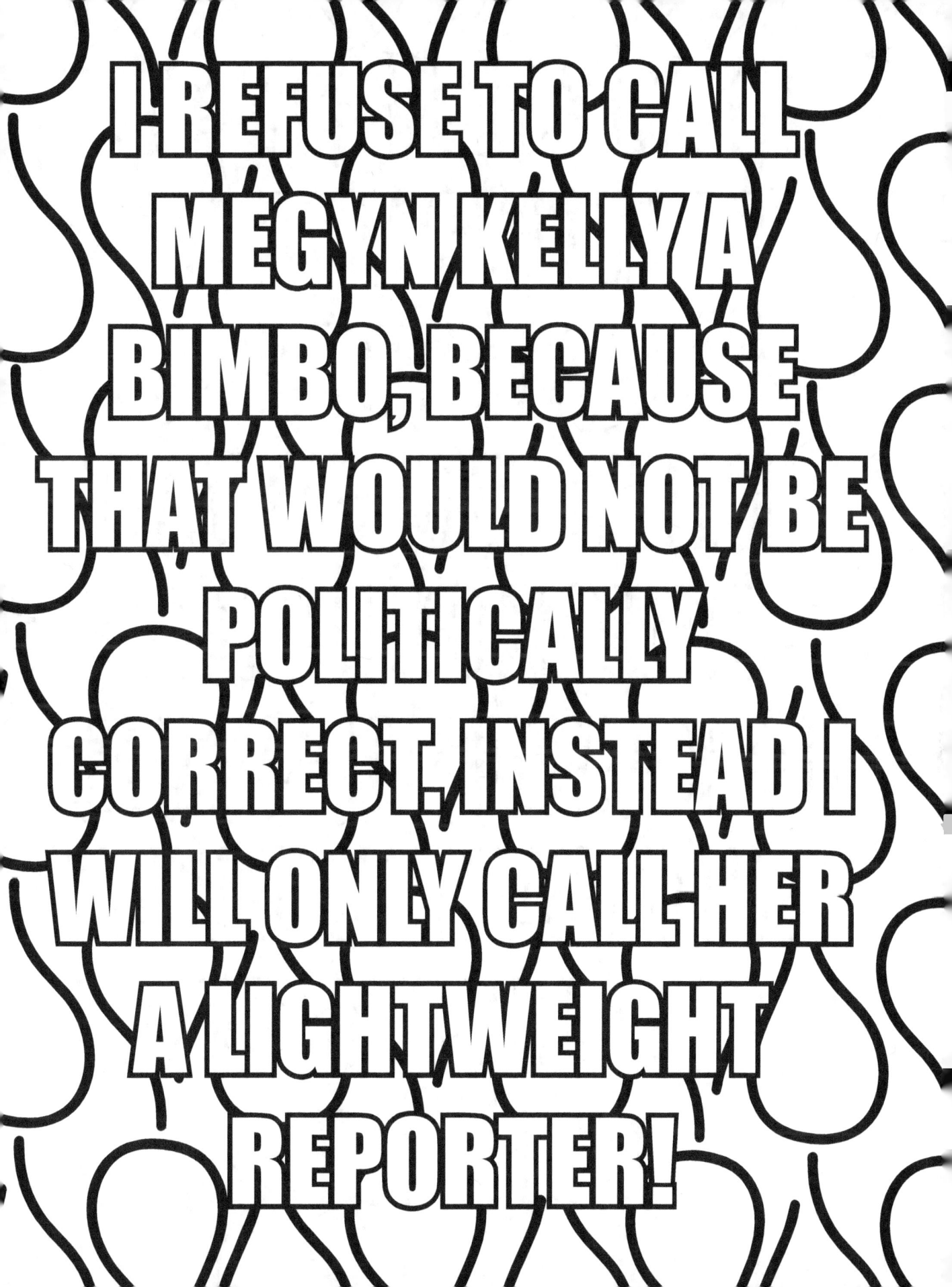

I REFUSE TO CALL MEGYN KELLY A BIMBO, BECAUSE THAT WOULD NOT BE POLITICALLY CORRECT. INSTEAD I WILL ONLY CALL HER A LIGHTWEIGHT REPORTER!

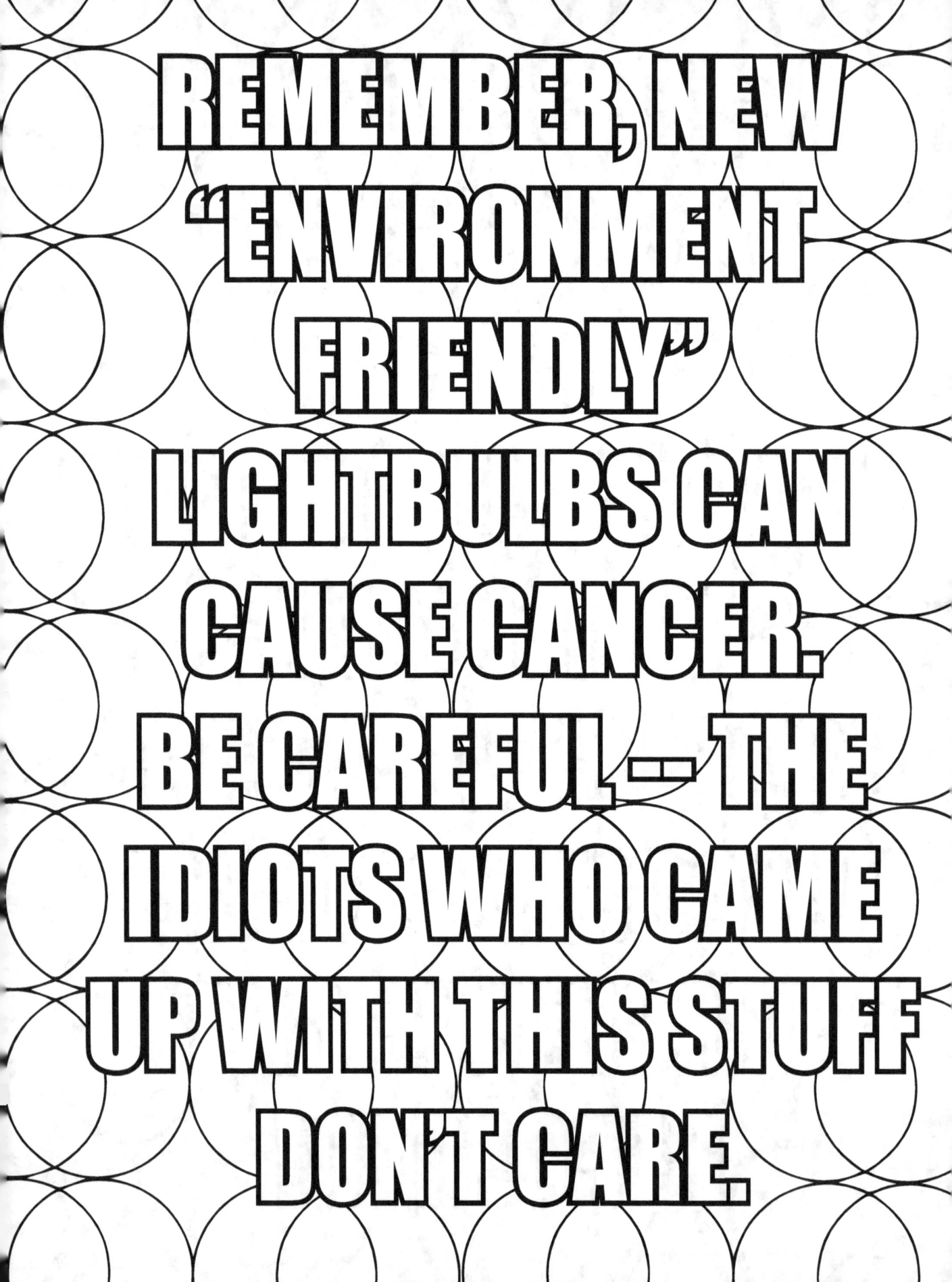

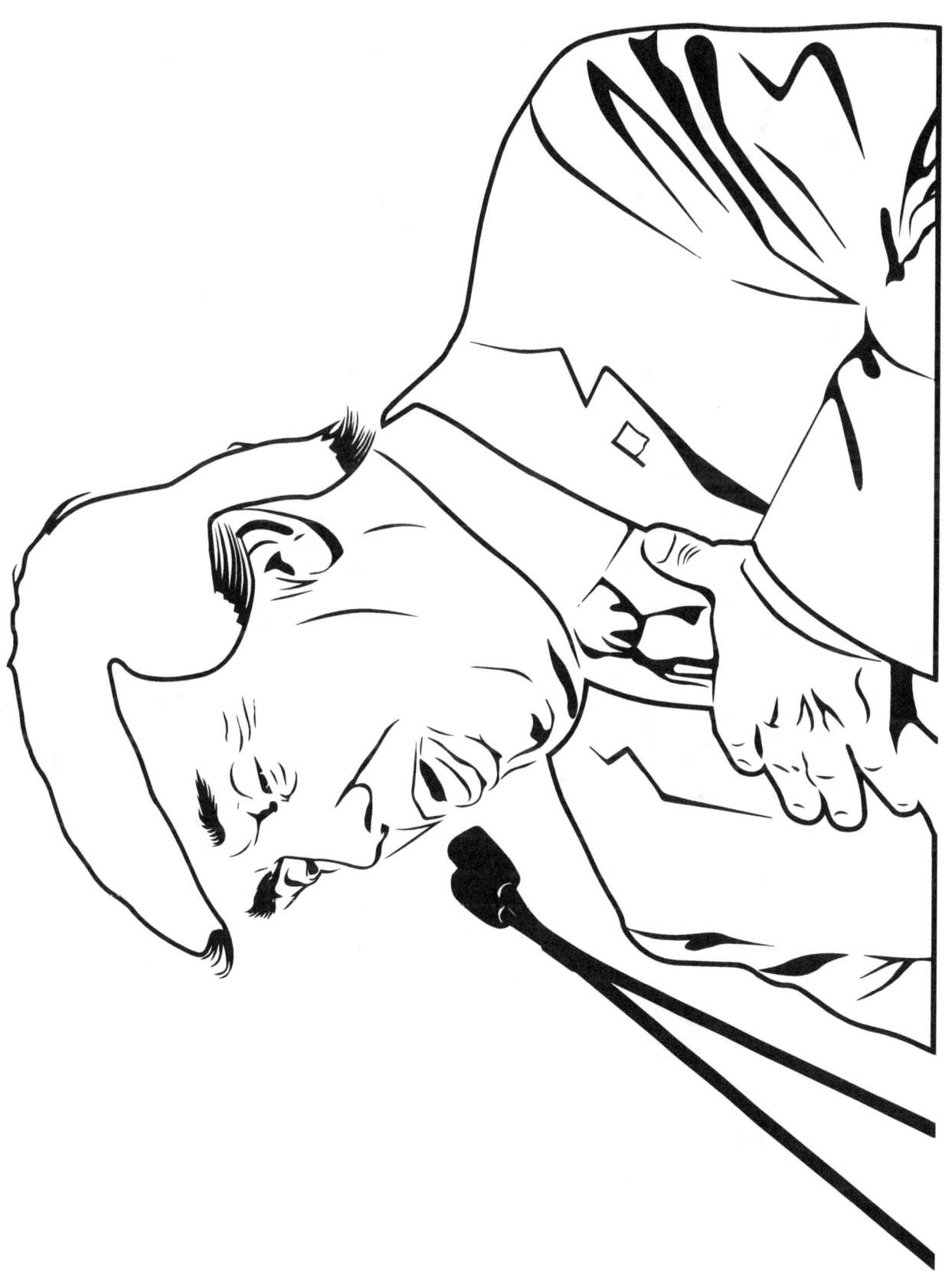

@ARIANNAHUFF IS UNATTRACTIVE BOTH INSIDE AND OUT. I FULLY UNDERSTAND WHY HER FORMER HUSBAND LEFT HER FOR A MAN - HE MADE A GOOD DECISION.

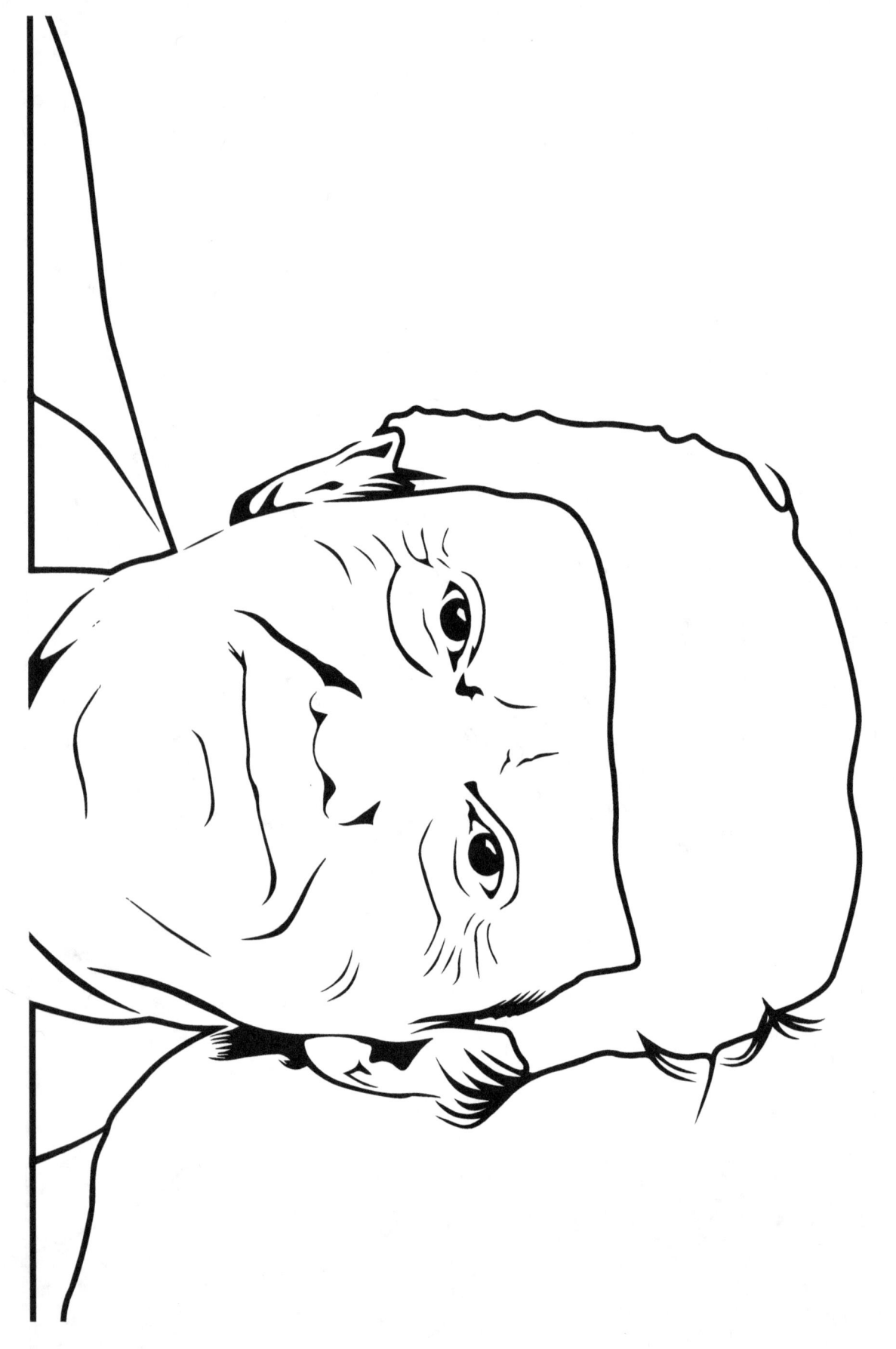

ENJOY ART THERAPY

DESIGNED IN AMSTERDAM